SPAM

SPAM®

CHOPPED PORK AND HAM

MINIMUM 90% PORK

THE COOKBOOK

Marguerite Patten

hamlyn

An Hachette UK Company
www.hachette.co.uk

First published in Great Britain in 2000 by
Hamlyn, a division of Octopus Publishing Group Ltd
2–4 Heron Quays, London E14 4JP
www.octopusbooksusa.com

This edition published in 2009

Distributed in the U.S. and Canada by Octopus Books USA:
c/o Hachette Book Group
237 Park Avenue
New York NY 10017

ISBN 978-0-600-62047-1

A CIP catalogue record for this book is available from the British Library

Printed and bound in China

10 9 8 7 6 5 4 3 2

The publishers have made every effort to contact copyright holders.
We apologise in advance for any potential omissions and ask anyone who
has not been properly credited to contact us so that we can update any
future editions.

Project Editor: Sarah Ford
Copy-editor: Anne Crane
Picture researcher: Rosie Garai

Home Economist: Dagmar Vesely

Notes

1 Standard level spoon measurements are used in all recipes.

    1 tablespoon = one 15 ml spoon
    1 tablespoon = one 1¼ American tablespoon
    1 teaspoon = one 5 ml spoon

2 Imperial, metric and American measurements have been given in all recipes.
Use one set of measurements only and not a mixture of both.

3 Measurements for canned food have been given as a standard metric
equivalent.

4 Eggs should be medium unless otherwise stated. The Department of Health
advises that eggs should not be consumed raw. This book contains dishes made
with raw or lightly cooked eggs. It is prudent for more vulnerable people, such as
pregnant and nursing mothers, invalids, the elderly, babies and young children, to
avoid uncooked or lightly cooked dishes made with eggs. Once prepared, these
dishes should be kept refrigerated and used promptly.

5 Milk should be full fat unless otherwise stated.

6 Once a can of SPAM has been opened it can be wrapped and stored in the
refrigerator for 2 days. Leftover SPAM can be frozen.

7 Fresh herbs should be used unless otherwise stated. If unavailable, use dried
herbs as an alternative, but halve the quantities stated.

8 Pepper should be freshly ground black pepper unless otherwise stated.

9 Ovens should be preheated to the specified temperature - if using a fan-
assisted oven, follow the manufacturer's instructions for adjusting the time and
the temperature.

10 This book includes dishes made with nuts and nut derivatives. It is advisable
for customers with known allergic reactions to nuts and nut derivatives and
those who may be potentially vulnerable to these allergies, such as pregnant and
nursing mothers, invalids, the elderly, babies and children, to avoid dishes made
with nuts and nut oils. It is also prudent to check the labels of pre-prepared
ingredients for the possible inclusion of nut derivatives.

Contents

SPAM is a registered trademark for chopped pork and ham owned by Hormel Foods Corporation.

Executive Art Editor: Leigh Jones

Photographer: Sean Myers
Stylist: Clare Hunt

Action Photographer: Anja Koch
Production Controller: Lisa Moore

®

Introduction

Love it or hate it, SPAM is one of only a tiny number of brand-name food products that everybody knows. From its humble beginnings in Austin, Minnesota, it has become a symbol of American culture, a powerful icon in both the USA and many other parts of the world. So great is its hold on the American people that it even features in the Smithsonian National Museum of American History. SPAM is as representative of American life as apple pie or Coca-Cola.

SPAM was first developed in the 1930s by Jay C. Hormel, president of Geo. A. Hormel & Co., as a way to use up the pork shoulder meat left over from the pork industry. This was good quality meat but was difficult to cut off the bone in decent-sized pieces. Its "leftover" status made it an unlikely basis for a new product, but the last 60 years have proved its success. It was slow to get started because the American housewife of the time had been brought up to believe that meat that had not been stored in a refrigerator could make you ill. But soon the idea of canned foods took hold and since then SPAM has not looked back .

SPAM first reached icon status during World War II when it fed the troops, often morning, noon, and night. It was one of the most widely used military foodstuffs among US troops, but allied troops also received SPAM in their rations, and it was used to feed starving Russians during the German occupation. SPAM soon developed a reputation among US service personnel, who ridiculed the product because they were served it at almost every meal. Although it got some bad press at the time, this only helped to make SPAM better known.

In wartime Britain, SPAM was an important part of the national diet, not only for the troops, but also for civilians, for whom it proved to be a great source of protein at a time when fresh meat was heavily rationed.

It became so famous that in the 1970s the British comedy team, Monty Python's Flying Circus, whose parents had eaten SPAM during the war years, wrote a skit about a restaurant featuring only SPAM dishes on its menu (see pages 34–35).

IMPORTANT NOTICE

"SPAM"

is the registered trademark distinguishing the product manufactured **exclusively** by Geo. A. Hormel & Co. "Spam" is made of pure pork shoulder meat with ham meat added. "Spam" is sold <u>ONLY</u> in 12 oz. tins plainly marked with the trademark "Spam." We are sorry that during the war supplies of "Spam" are restricted.

GEO. A. HORMEL & CO.
AUSTIN, MINNESOTA, U.S.A.
*"Spam" is a registered trademark.

Over the years SPAM has beaten off its many competitors and imitators and still prospers to this day as an all-American product, one that has been kind to the 1600 Austin residents who work for Hormel Foods, LLC., as well as the meat processors and hog farmers who make a living from it. SPAM is so much part of the town's identity (Hormel Foods helped to build the hospital and library and donates generously to local charities) that Austin is now officially known as SPAM Town, USA, and uses this honorable title to promote itself.

SPAM is sold in virtually every grocery store in America – about 90 million cans a year. The Hawaiians are obsessed with SPAM, consuming over twice the national average, about four cans of SPAM per person every year. They especially love their favorite pork product in sushi – SPAM musubi, a rice cake topped with pickled plum, a slice of fried SPAM, and wrapped with nori seaweed. This dish even rivals pizza as the school cafeteria favorite.

SPAM is now sold all over the world and, as an American product, it has great prestige in many societies, and is considered on a par with

Left: Putting SPAM on a pedestal – the Austin, Minnesota tourism campaign – a giant SPAM can building.

Below: SPAM spans the globe proving to be popular with the Japanese.

Right: The fastest SPAM can in the world, SPAM hits the race track in style.

Far Right: Taste the fun, SPAM fans enjoy one of Hormel's many organized promotional events.

and is often presented as a gift, like luxury chocolates and fine wines. Guam has a huge appetite for SPAM, its citizens consuming on average eight cans of SPAM per person per year.

SPAM is not just about food, however, it's also about fun. Over the years hundreds of fan clubs have sprung up all over the USA. In 1998 they were organized into the Official SPAM Fan Club (see page 57) by Hormel Foods, LLC. In return for membership privileges, members

baseball caps and McDonald's. South Korea is one of the most rapidly expanding markets. Here SPAM is considered a gourmet luxury

must "defend the good name of SPAM luncheon meat, enjoy the great taste of SPAM, and spread the good tidings of SPAM to all corners of the sandwich."

Every year there are SPAM festivals all over the USA with recipe competitions, dressing up, and SPAM sculpting events. SPAM has a huge following on the web, with hundreds of web-sites dedicated to the appreciation of SPAM.

And now, by popular demand, Hormel offers non-meat products to their SPAM fans, such as SPAM boxer shorts, SPAM sandals that stamp SPAM wherever you go, SPAM Christmas tree ornaments, and even SPAM babywear for its younger fans. However, it is the T-shirts, ear-rings, and neckties that are among the biggest selling SPAM products.

Despite all the jokes and fun surrounding it, SPAM has a very real place in the hearts of Americans. For many it is the nostalgia, the comforting thought that SPAM has been around since their childhood and, in this ever-changing world, is pretty much exactly the same now as when they first tasted it. They can open a can to find the same reliably moist, fla-vorsome, and lightly spiced meat inside. For others it holds the same attraction as it always has for housewives all over the USA – it is convenient, it is nutritious, and it is an extreme-ly versatile product. But best of all, you don't need to be able to cook to make a tasty meal out of SPAM.

9

SPAM®: THE HISTORY

The blend of chopped pork and ham that has become famous under the name of SPAM luncheon meat was created and produced by the Geo. A. Hormel company of Austin, Minnesota, USA. The person responsible for its development was the president of the company, Jay C. Hormel, son of the founder, George, who had created this large and prosperous company from his modest beginnings as a retail butcher. Jay had shown business acumen from his schooldays and brought many new ideas to the firm. When planning SPAM he envisaged a vastly superior canned luncheon meat based mainly on ground shoulder of prime pork.

At first father George was not impressed with the idea but his son persisted in experiments to achieve a first-class product. He wanted one that was full of flavor, that could be an acceptable alternative to fresh meat, but also would side-step the fluctuating prices and storage problems associated with fresh pork. Jay had already had experience of producing various forms of canned foods, including large cans of ham and spiced ham for butchers and delicatessen shops. The drawback to these was, once opened, the meat had a limited shelf life, even when refrigerated. Traders would slice the amounts required by various customers but had to store the remainder. This made Jay realize that if his new vision of canned meat was to be the success he hoped, the meat had to be canned in small domestic-sized containers.

Various experts on canning were brought in to work on the project. The aim was to produce a firm textured, cooked pork luncheon meat that looked attractive, tasted good and could be served cold from the can or heated in various ways like fresh meat. One of the initial problems was to make sure there was no liquid (loose juice) in the cans.

It is believed that Jean Vernet, the French chef employed by the Hormel company, played a major part in formulating the final flavor of the product.

With all technical difficulties resolved one can imagine everyone's delight when the new product was ready to launch. There was however one problem – **what was it to be called?** Originally it was known as chopped ham but a catchier name was required.

SPAM®

ED PORK AND HAM

The Christening of SPAM®

This lack of name caused considerable delay before the canned luncheon meat appeared on the market. Various names were suggested but none seemed appropriate. It had to be a brand name that could not be copied by competitors. By late 1936 there was a satisfactory product – ready to be sold – but one without a name.

It is reported that Jay Hormel decided to stage a New Year's party for the express purpose of naming "his baby". Guests were to be entitled to a drink for each name they suggested and there would be a prize of $100 for the winner. The host is believed to have commented at a later date that "by the fourth drink people began to show some imagination."

The name SPAM was suggested by Kenneth Daigneau, brother of the Hormel vice-president and an actor, who was a guest at the party. He had appeared in various shows on stage and on the radio but certainly was not of star status. However he did choose a wonderfully apt star name for the new luncheon meat and one that was accepted by the firm. SPAM was a short word that everyone would remember; it was easy to pronounce and it described the contents of the can with its combination of **shoulder of pork and ham**.

Above: Jay C. Hormel with his many Hormel products.

Right: Kenneth Daigneau who famously gave SPAM a name.

11

SPAM®'s Launch

SPAM was launched in the USA in May 1937, and began to sell well in spite of the fact that within a short time there were over one hundred competitors. Many of these disappeared in record time, due to their lack of quality. Because SPAM was an inexpensive meat it meant that even poor families could afford to buy it. By 1938 it had become so popular that it received an award for the best company development of 1937.

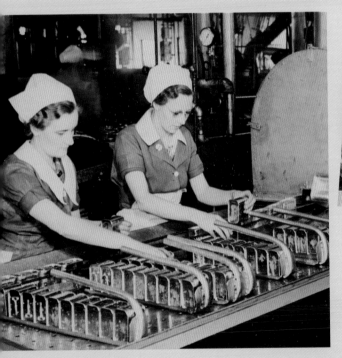

Americans were becoming accustomed to television advertising at this time and SPAM commercials were shown on various popular programs. SPAM featured in the lyric of the first singing TV advertisement to the tune of 'My Bonny Lies over the Ocean'.

This page and opposite: Early pictures from the Hormel Food Corporation's archives.

Wartime America

In March 1941, Congress passed the Lend-Lease Act which provided aid to the Allied Forces, and many firms, including Hormel, moved into wartime production. SPAM was one of the foods that was sent to Britain for civilians and members of the armed forces. It was also dispatched to the many countries where men and women were serving. When Germany invaded Russia, SPAM helped to feed the hard-pressed people.

Russia's Nikita Kruschev once said "Without SPAM, we wouldn't have been able to feed our army".

After Pearl Harbor, the US joined the Allies, and American forces served in many parts of the world; SPAM was needed to feed them. Service personnel are not always complimentary about their food and some GIs formed a less than flattering opinion of SPAM. Obviously the dishes of which it formed a part were often fairly dull, due to the primitive conditions under which they were prepared. Sometimes shortages of alternative foods meant that SPAM was served for breakfast, lunch and dinner on the same day – few people would be delighted at that monotonous menu!

Some complaints may have been caused by the fact that there was a special American Government brand of SPAM, prepared by Hormel, but without the superior flavor of true SPAM. This may well have caused adverse reports about the luncheon meat. You will find some of the comments from GIs and other service personnel on the pages that follow.

Wartime Memories

Irena Urdang de Tour called the packages of SPAM, chocolate and soup she received in the ruins of Warsaw after years of slave labour in Berlin "ambrosia".

Some enterprising GIs would trade their cans of SPAM from home for rum or cigarettes. Servicemen from Britain and Canada looked with envy at the generous amounts of food sent to the Americans.

At one period in the United States there was a tin shortage and a ban on the domestic sale of most brand products made by the Hormel firm – except SPAM.

In a letter to Jay Hormel, Mrs. Amelia A. Garrett of London praised "the best tinned food that I have tasted in two wars ... It's 100 per cent perfect nourishment and tasty".

Some members of the American forces complained bitterly that they were fed SPAM by the forces' cooks and had cans of SPAM sent from home – as a treat!

SPAM® Fact

Between 1939 and 1942 the sales of SPAM® doubled, and by 1944 90 per cent of all Hormel canned foods were exported to various theaters of war.

Wartime Britain

The USA's Lend-Lease was a wonderful help to beleaguered Britain. Among the foods we received was concentrated orange juice; this was given to expectant mothers, babies and young children and played an important role in promoting good health, for it was a valuable source of vitamin C. Fresh citrus fruits were not available between 1939 and 1945, for all vital shipping space was needed to transport men and military equipment.

In Britain fresh meat was so scarce that from time to time corned beef (often called bully beef) had to form part of the official meat ration. Men and women serving abroad also had corned beef with unwelcome regularity, so both civilians and members of the forces welcomed the new meat by the name of SPAM. Because it came in cans it was easy and safe to transport throughout Britain and to many places further afield.

One of the wartime measures instituted by the British Government was the provision of midday meals for school children. This helped to ensure that growing children had as much nutritious food as was possible in those days. School caterers, like all cooks of the time, had to plan meals with restricted ingredients, so SPAM figured largely in the menus and it proved very popular with the children.

More Wartime Memories

Mr. H. Ranfield was a prisoner of war in Germany at Stalag Luft 7. The prisoners enjoyed eating SPAM and they also used the cans. They beat these flat with spoons and used them for dispensing trays in the medical rooms.

Mr. G. Holley served in India during the war. He had beans and corned beef twice a day for much of the time. One day a US Officer appeared with a truck load of SPAM to exchange for the corned beef. The exchange was a success. The American GIs had corned beef – a change for them – and the British enjoyed the new flavor of SPAM. Mr. Holley stills likes SPAM today – but not corned beef.

Mrs. E. Bowie remembers sitting in an air-raid shelter eating her mother's homemade SPAM sandwiches. She says they went down a treat and even made the family forget about the bombs dropping outside.

Mr. T. Howard spent his time in the war in the Merchant Navy on a small coaster. They had no refrigeration for fresh meat, so they had SPAM fried for breakfast, cold with salad for lunch and with mashed potatoes for dinner. Modern ships have refrigeration but still serve SPAM.

A meaty subject...

She needs as much meat as he does!

Do heavy workers need more meat?
No. Daily wear and tear on the tissues is not materially affected by the kind of work done.

Madam – important notice!

"SPAM" – is the registered trade-mark distinguishing the product manufactured exclusively by Geo. A. Hormel & Co., "Spam" is made of pure pork shoulder meat with ham meat added. "Spam" is sold ONLY in 12 oz. tins plainly marked with the trademark "Spam." We are sorry that during the war, supplies of "Spam" are restricted.

"SPAM"
* "Spam" is a registered trademark.

SPAM® Fact

At the end of the war in 1945, SPAM® was sent to help feed the starving people of Europe.

SPAM® – THE RECIPES
All Day Dish

SPAM luncheon meat is a most versatile food. It can be sliced, diced, or mashed according to the way you would like to serve it. Modern SPAM retains all the fine qualities of the luncheon meat that was first launched in 1937. In addition to classic SPAM there is now SPAMLITE which has 25 per cent less fat and salt. You can use this or ordinary SPAM in all recipes in the book. The SPAM can of today has changed – no longer is there a key to open it but instead an easy-to-pull ring on the top.

When can you serve SPAM? The answer is whenever you like – SPAM can be enjoyed at any time of the day, from breakfast to a sustaining dinner or a light late-night snack.

Breakfast SPAM®: Heat a very little oil in a frying pan. Fry slices of SPAM until piping hot then top with fried eggs. Serve with grilled or fried tomatoes and mushrooms.

Croque Monsieur: Make sandwiches of sliced SPAM and sliced Swiss or other good cooking cheese. Quickly dip them into beaten egg, then fry until crisp and brown on both sides.

SPAM® Rarebit: Top slices of toast with sliced SPAM, then cover these with grated or sliced Cheddar or other hard cheese. Place under a preheated broiler and heat until the cheese is bubbling and golden brown. To make a more substantial meal, serve the rarebit with tomatoes.

SPAM®

CHOPPED PORK AND HAM

18

Super Sandwiches

Sandwiches are quick to make, easy to serve and make a nutritious meal to eat at home, at school or work, or to take on a picnic. Today sandwiches can be made more interesting with a choice of modern breads, such as ciabatta or focaccia loaves. SPAM® sandwiches achieved fame during the Second World War. Here are some suggested fillings based on SPAM. The proportion of the various ingredients is a matter of personal choice.

Breakfast Special: Sliced SPAM, scrambled egg, sliced tomatoes, and watercress or arugula sprigs.

Oriental Treat: Mix mashed SPAM with a little crushed then chopped lemon grass, chopped cilantro, and a sprinkling of dried coconut. Add a very few drops of soy sauce. Top with bean sprouts or some Napa cabbage.

Full of Crunch: Mix mashed SPAM with finely chopped dessert apple, finely chopped celery, and chopped green bell pepper.

Hot and Spicy: Mash SPAM with a few drops of Tabasco or chili sauce or a good pinch of chili powder, add well-drained and slightly crushed red kidney beans, and skinned chopped tomatoes.

Salad Special: Fill the sandwiches with various kinds of lettuce, sliced SPAM, rings of green bell pepper, slices of tomato and cucumber.

Sweet and Sour: Drain sweetened canned pineapple rings, then chop them up finely, and slice some pickled sweet dill pickles. Mix the pineapple and dill pickles with mashed SPAM. Top with crisp lettuce.

SPAM® for Parties

Here are some interesting party 'nibbles' that can be prepared within minutes.

Crudités with Savory Dip: To make the crudités, prepare a selection of raw vegetables, e.g. narrow strips of green, yellow and red bell pepper, baby carrots, neat pieces of celery, and cauliflower flowerets. To make the dip, put 7 ounces SPAM® into a food processor with ⅔ cup tomato juice and 1 teaspoon Worcestershire sauce and puree until smooth. If preferred, simply mash the SPAM, then gradually add the tomato juice and Worcestershire sauce. Tip the dip into a bowl, stir in 2 tablespoons finely chopped chives, 1 tablespoon finely chopped cilantro, 1 teaspoon prepared mustard, and salt and pepper if desired. To serve, spoon the dip into an attractive small bowl and place in the center of a large platter, with the crudités arranged around it.
Serves 4–5

Stuffed Celery: Mash 4 ounces SPAM in a bowl with ½ cup soft cream cheese, or cottage cheese. Add 1 tablespoon finely chopped nuts. Cut about 20 short lengths of crisp celery and fill the cavities with the SPAM mixture. Top with nuts and/or small pieces of black and green olives.
Makes 20

SPAM®, Apricot and Coconut Balls: Mash 7 ounces SPAM. Cut ⅓ cup ready-to-eat dried apricots into very small pieces, add to the SPAM and knead well. Form the mixture into small balls. Put 3 tablespoons dried coconut on a plate and roll the small balls in this until well coated. Push a toothpick through each ball.
Makes 15–18
Variations: Add 1 teaspoon curry paste to the mixture.
• Use prunes instead of apricots.

SPAM® Fact

In Korea, SPAM® is sold in stylish presentation gift boxes with eight cans in each one.

Cheese Fondue

This makes an ideal party dish. Squares of SPAM and fresh bread or toast are dipped into the creamy cheese mixture. If you do not possess a proper fondue heater and pot, you can use a heat-resistant bowl placed over a pan of simmering water to melt the cheese. The recipe uses the two classic cheeses but any good cooking cheese, such as Cheddar, can be used. The cornstarch is not essential but it helps to prevent the mixture separating.

Preparation time: 10 minutes
Cooking time: 10–15 minutes
Serves 4

1 tablespoon butter, softened
1 garlic clove, halved
1 teaspoon cornstarch
1¼ cups dry white wine
2 cups Gruyère or Emmenthal cheese, grated
2 cups Swiss cheese, grated
1–2 tablespoons kirsch or brandy (optional)
salt and white pepper
Dippers:
SPAM®, cut into 1-inch cubes
fresh bread or toast, cut into 1-inch cubes

1 Spread or brush the butter around the inside of a ceramic fondue pot (this is more suitable for a cheese fondue than a metal pot, which can become too hot) and then rub with the garlic clove.

2 Blend the cornstarch with the wine, and add to the pot with the cheeses. Heat gently over the fondue heater, stirring occasionally.

3 Season to taste with salt and pepper, then add the kirsch or brandy, if using. Serve with the dippers, which should be speared on fondue or ordinary forks.

Variations: SPAM® Fondue: Heat cubes of SPAM in hot oil then drain on paper towels. Serve dipped in tomato ketchup or mayonnaise. Never try to eat the very hot meat on forks that have been dipped in the oil – they become ultra hot.

Did you know?

SPAM® is sold in 50 countries around the world? For more details, see page 47.

21

SPAM® & Mushroom Ramekins

Preparation time: 10 minutes
Cooking time: 12–15 minutes
Serves 4–6

2 cups small white mushrooms, finely chopped
7 ounces SPAM®, finely chopped
2 tablespoons freshly grated Parmesan cheese
1 tablespoon finely chopped parsley
1 egg, beaten
⅓ cup light cream
1 tablespoon chopped lemon grass (optional)
salt and pepper
flat-leaf parsley, to garnish

1 Grease 4–6 individual ovenproof soufflé dishes. Mix together all the ingredients and spoon into the dishes. Bake in a preheated oven, 400°F, for 12 minutes or until just firm, then garnish with parsley and serve.

Variations: SPAM® and Egg Ramekins: Omit the mushrooms in the main recipe. Mix together all the ingredients, place in the dishes, then break a small egg into each one. Top with a few drops of oil and a sprinkling of Parmesan. Bake as in the main recipe.

• For a softer set egg, bake the SPAM mixture for 5 minutes then add the eggs and topping, return to the oven, and continue cooking for a further 7–10 minutes.

Did you know?

That sprinkling a little salt on the board makes it easier to chop or crush garlic.

22

Savoury Cheesecake

Preparation time: 25 minutes, plus cooling
Cooking time: 1¼ hours
Serves 6–8

Crumb crust:
⅓ cup butter, melted
1 teaspoon grated lemon zest
2 teaspoons chopped parsley
1½ cups Graham crackers, crushed
salt and pepper

Topping:
2 cups low-fat cottage cheese or pot cheese
8 ounces SPAM®, very finely chopped
1 teaspoon grated lemon zest
2 teaspoons chopped cilantro
2 tablespoons finely chopped chives
1 tablespoon chopped parsley
½ cup carrots, finely grated
¼ cup cornstarch
3 large eggs, whisked
2 tablespoons milk or lemon juice
salt and pepper

1 Grease a 9–10-inch springform pan or a cake pan with a loose base. Mix all the ingredients for the crumb crust and press the mixture into the bottom of the pan.

2 To make the topping, beat the cottage cheese well then gradually add all the other topping ingredients. Season to taste with salt and pepper, then spoon the topping over the crumb crust. Bake in a preheated oven, 300°F, for about 1¼ hours, or until firm. Leave the cheesecake to cool in the oven with the heat off (to prevent wrinkling). Keep the door of an electric oven ajar, as it will retain heat. When the cheesecake is cold, remove it from the pan.

3 The cheesecake can be garnished in various ways, such as dill sprigs, a border of finely chopped SPAM, rings of cooked carrot, radish 'roses', sliced tomatoes or a piped border of cream cheese with small pieces of red and green bell peppers and sprigs of parsley and cilantro.

SPAM® Porcupine

Cut the SPAM into slices just over ½ inch thick, then cut the slices into neat dice. Thread the dice on to toothpicks with some of the following ingredients

- baby cocktail onions
- small sweet dill pickles or diced cucumber
- halved canned pineapple cubes or diced fresh pineapple
- segments of ripe avocado, dipped in lemon juice
- maraschino or candied cherries.

SPAM is sufficiently firm to allow the sticks to be pushed through the meat without breaking. It is also pleasantly moist and enhances the flavor of the other ingredients. Press the selection of miniature kebabs into a small red or green cabbage or a large grapefruit. The cabbage or grapefruit can be used afterwards.

The cocktail bites can be served with various hot or cold dips, such as

- pesto
- tomato ketchup blended with a little thick yogurt or fromage frais plus a few drops of soy or Worcestershire sauce
- mashed avocado blended with lemon juice and yogurt
- thick tomato purée with a dash of Tabasco sauce or pinch of chili powder.

SPAM® Fact

If all the cans of SPAM ever eaten were put end-to-end, they would circle the globe at least ten times.

SPAMtastic™ Snacks

Very often one does not require a full meal, but prefers to eat a quick snack instead. On many of these occasions you will find SPAM makes a good choice. It is a wholesome food that provides a generous supply of protein as well as some fat and carbohydrate.

Today, at the start of a new millennium, there are genuine worries that many people, including children, are eating less nutritious foods than they should. Often the household starts the day without any breakfast – why?

There isn't time!

I can't face it.

are just two of the reasons given. On page 18 you will find some easy ideas for breakfast. These do require a short cooking time. If that is a problem, why not adopt the habit that is so popular in Scandinavia and other European countries and serve a plate of sliced meat (including SPAM) and cheese. This is ready in seconds.

Although it sounds harmless to leave home without eating breakfast, in fact it is not a good thing. It has been shown that physically and mentally we achieve less and often develop a slightly 'sinking' feeling during the middle of the morning. That is when we tend to indulge in sweet snacks which are high in sugar but have very little nutritional value.

Many children and adults take a packed meal to school or work. Sandwiches are a good choice (see page 19 and below), but there are other suggestions given on page 32. These are equally suitable for TV snacks – easy to eat while watching your favorite programs.

Sandwich Kebabs: Make sandwiches with the fillings given on page 19 but use different breads. Cut the sandwiches into bite-sized pieces and thread on to skewers.

Rolled Sandwiches: Roll thin crustless bread and butter around the fillings.

The Poets Speak

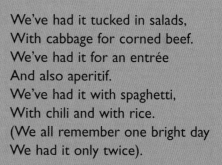

I was intrigued by the flights of fancy produced by various poets to describe, laud or decry SPAM. These are taken from the fascinating book *SPAM — A Biography* by Carolyn Wyman. From Weird Al we have two verses on SPAM and I quote one of these.

> If you're running low, go to the store,
> Carry some money, to help you buy more,
> The tab is there, to open the can,
> The can is there, to hold in the SPAM.

The following verse from Moe Tucker is in calypso rhythm.

> I'm goin' to work
> Little baby, baby
> I'm goin' to work
> Today.
> Mama's going to make
> A dollar, dollar
> And buy some SPAM
> Today.

From less than happy service personnel there were several stanzas — not very complimentary in most cases. I quote my two favorites.

> We've had it tucked in salads,
> With cabbage for corned beef.
> We've had it for an entrée
> And also aperitif.
> We've had it with spaghetti,
> With chili and with rice.
> (We all remember one bright day
> We had it only twice).
>
> Back home I have an angel
> Whose name I want to change.
> I'll purchase her a fancy home
> With a brand-new modern range;
> But marital bliss is sure to cease
> If I ever ask for ham
> And find my eggs are looking up
> For a gol-darned slice of SPAM.

SPAM® Caesar Salad

The addition of diced SPAM makes this salad more interesting and sustaining. Plain or garlic croutons are readily available in supermarkets, but instructions for preparing them are given below. They may be frozen on flat trays, then packed into rigid, freezerproof containers.

Preparation time: 12 minutes
Serves 4

1 garlic clove, halved
1 crisp lettuce, preferably romaine
7 ounces SPAM®, cut into small dice
about 16 plain or garlic croutons (see below)
Dressing:
1 garlic clove, crushed or chopped
1 teaspoon prepared mustard
2 tablespoons extra virgin olive oil
1–2 teaspoons Worcestershire sauce
1 tablespoon lemon juice
1 tablespoon mayonnaise
3 tablespoons freshly grated Parmesan cheese
salt and pepper

1 Rub the garlic around the sides of a salad bowl. Place the lettuce leaves in the bowl with half the diced SPAM. Mix together all the ingredients for the dressing.

2 Just before serving, toss the lettuce and SPAM in the dressing. Top with the remaining SPAM and the croutons.

Plain croutons: Cut 2 slices of crustless bread into ¼–½-inch dice. Heat 2 tablespoons oil in a skillet and fry the bread until crisp and golden. Drain on paper towels.

Garlic croutons: Heat 2 tablespoons oil with 2–3 halved garlic cloves for 1 minute. Set aside for 15 minutes for the flavor to develop, then proceed as for plain croutons.

Swedish SPAM®salat

Preparation time: 20 minutes, plus standing
Serves 4–6

2 tablespoons white wine vinegar

1 beet, cooked and cut into 1-inch dice

1 large dessert apple, cored but not peeled and cut into
    1-inch dice

4–5 potatoes, cooked and cut into 1-inch dice

12 ounces SPAM®, cut into 1-inch dice

3 tablespoons mayonnaise

2 teaspoons capers

1 tablespoon lemon juice

2 small sweet dill pickles, thinly sliced

2 tablespoons chopped scallions

To garnish:

mixed lettuce leaves

chopped dill

2–3 hard-cooked eggs, quartered

1 Pour the vinegar into a large bowl, add the beet and diced apple and let stand for about 10 minutes.

2 Add all the remaining ingredients to the beet and apple. Mix well, then either leave in this bowl or transfer to a smaller one. Cover the salad with a plate and a small weight and leave in the refrigerator for 1½–2 hours.

3 To serve, turn out the salad on to a bed of lettuce, top with the dill, and arrange the quartered eggs around the edge.

SPAM® Fact

You now have the choice of SPAM® or SPAM LITE®.

Tortilla

This Spanish omelet tastes equally good hot or cold, so it makes a good snack for picnics or part of a packed meal. As it is not folded but served flat, make it in a 7–8 inch omelet pan or a skillet.

Preparation time: 15 minutes
Cooking time: 13 minutes
Serves 2

1 tablespoon olive oil
1 small onion, finely chopped
1 potato, cooked and cut into ¼-inch dice
4 ounces SPAM®, cut into ¼-inch dice
4 large eggs, beaten
2 tablespoons butter
1 tablespoon chopped parsley
salt and pepper
chopped chives, to garnish

1 Heat the oil in a 7–8-inch pan, add the onion, and cook for 5 minutes. Add the potato and SPAM, cook for 3 minutes, then tip into the bowl with the beaten eggs. Season with salt and pepper and mix well.

2 Heat the butter in the pan, add the egg mixture and parsley, and cook until the tortilla is firm. Slide it on to a plate, cut into wedges, and garnish with chopped chives.

Variations: Instead of cooking the onion, heat thinly sliced scallions with the potato and SPAM. These add a touch of crispness to the tortilla.
• **Pepper Tortilla:** Add a little chopped raw or cooked red and/or green bell pepper and/or cooked peas to the potato and SPAM.
• **SPAM® Omelet:** Add ¼ cup finely diced SPAM for every 2 eggs. Cook in the usual way. Chopped cilantro adds color and flavor.

Cooking Tip

Tortilla and other omelets can be cooked in suitable dishes in the microwave.

Bread and SPAM®

We are fortunate nowadays that good bakers and supermarkets sell a wide range of breads. Several of these offer a great variety for making interesting snacks.

FROM FRANCE
Baguette Sandwiches: Split short thin French loaves lengthways. Spread the cut surfaces with a very little butter (this can be flavored with Dijon mustard). Sandwich the two halves together with sliced SPAM, chopped black olives, crisp lettuce, and sliced tomatoes. Cut into thick segments to serve.
• The SPAM® Pâté on page 43 may be spread on the bread instead of butter.

FROM ITALY
SPAM® and Pepper Bruschetta: Halve and seed red, green, and yellow bell peppers. Place under a preheated broiler with the rounded sides uppermost and heat until the skins blacken. Put into a plastic bag until cold, then strip away the skins and cut the peppers into segments. Place the segments on a piece of foil on the broiler pan, brush with a little oil, and heat for several minutes, then set aside. Toast 6 slices of ciabatta bread, rub with a cut garlic clove, and moisten with olive oil. Top the bread with slices

of SPAM, then with the cooked peppers. Heat for 2–3 minutes, then serve.

SPAM® Crostini: Prepare the 6 slices of ciabatta bread (see Bruschetta, left). Mash 7 ounces SPAM, mix with 2 tablespoons chopped sun-dried tomatoes, 2 tablespoons chopped green olives, and spread on the toast. Top with a generous layer of freshly grated Parmesan cheese, then brown under the broiler.

FROM GREECE
Savory Pita Breads: Dice some SPAM, mix with a little mayonnaise, then add some pine nuts, a good pinch of ground cumin, and a pinch of ground cinnamon. Fill the pockets in pita breads with lettuce, sliced tomatoes, and a little feta cheese, then top with the SPAM mixture.

Children in the Kitchen

Many children enjoy helping in the kitchen and creating special dishes. Children with poor and finicky appetites may well be inclined to eat better if they have assisted in preparing the dish. A number of the recipes on the previous pages are very easy for children to make and so are SPAMBURGER™s – a favorite snack – which follows on this page. SPAMBURGER™s are perfect for their school lunchboxes – or to serve at any time. They can be made suitable for lunch or dinner if served with an interesting salad or vegetables, rather than in a hamburger bun.

Obviously younger children should not attempt to open cans of food, or slice or chop ingredients without an older person being on hand to help them. Neither should they deal with very hot pans of food.

SPAMBURGER™s

Split soft hamburger rolls and fill them with crisp lettuce, tomato slices, then thick slices of SPAM® and slices of cheese. Rings of mild (red) onion and tomato ketchup may be added, or use a small amount of a favorite chutney.

Variations: Hot SPAMBURGER™s: Broil or fry the slices of SPAM, then add to the other ingredients and serve at once.

• **Crunchy SPAMBURGER™s:** Mash SPAM and mix with finely chopped red and/or green bell pepper, sliced scallions, and a very little fresh tomato purée or tomato ketchup. Form into round or square burgers and serve.

• **Fruity SPAMBURGER™s:** Omit the cheese, add rings of fresh or well-drained canned pineapple or dessert apple rings (dipped in lemon juice to keep them a good color).

• **Nutty SPAMBURGER™s:** Spread the split buns with peanut butter and add chopped nuts to mashed SPAM, then shape and put into the burger buns. Make sure no one is allergic to nuts.

Monty Python and SPAM®

Monty Python's Flying Circus was an exceptionally popular television series in the 1970s. The humor was so clever and unusual; of all the sketches, the one which highlighted SPAM was one of the most memorable. To remind older readers of the episode, and to introduce younger ones, I give a brief extract from that special program.

Imagine a café where, for some unknown reason, the rest of the customers seated were Vikings.

Enter Mr. and Mrs. Bun – not by the door – but flying on wires. They sit down at a table.

Mr. Bun Morning.

Waitress Morning.

Mr. Bun What have you got then?

Waitress Well, there's egg and bacon; egg, sausage and bacon; egg and Spam; egg, bacon and Spam; egg, bacon, sausage and Spam; Spam, bacon, sausage and Spam; Spam, egg, Spam, Spam, bacon and Spam; Spam, Spam; egg and Spam; Spam, Spam, Spam; Spam, Spam, Spam, baked beans, Spam, Spam, Spam and Spam; or a lobster thermidor aux crevettes with a Mornay sauce garnished with truffle pâté, brandy and a fried egg on top and Spam.

Mrs. Bun Have you got anything without Spam in it?

Waitress Well, Spam, egg, sausage and Spam. That's not got much Spam in it.

Mrs. Bun I don't want any Spam.

Mr. Bun Why can't she have egg, bacon, Spam and sausage?

Mrs. Bun That's got Spam in it!

Mr. Bun Not as much as Spam, egg, sausage and Spam.

Mrs. Bun Look, could I have egg, bacon, Spam and sausage without the Spam?

Waitress Uuuuuuuuuuugggh!

Mrs. Bun What d'you mean, uuugggh? I don't like Spam!

Vikings (singing) Spam, Spam, Spam, Spam.

Spam, Spam, Spam, Spam. Lovely Spam, wonderful Spam.
(Brief stock shot of a Viking Ship)
Lovely Spam, wonderful Spam . . .
Waitress Shut up! Shut up! Shut up! You can't have egg, bacon, Spam and sausage without the Spam.

The sketch continues with the waitress and the Buns becoming more and more hysterical and concludes with the Vikings singing the SPAM song, a visit by a **Hungarian,** then a visit by a **policeman** and then a **Historian** who announces that the Vikings had won another great victory and explains their military strategy in pompous detail, using a map with arrows on it. Within a few minutes, he too is infected by the atmosphere of the café and can say nothing but Spam, Spam, Spam, Spam . . .

At the time of the program it reminded the British of the SPAM they liked so much (or so little in some cases). What an outstanding advertisement for a product!

SPAM® for Lunch

Busy people will find SPAM an ideal food on which to base lunch dishes. This section starts with suggestions for eating outdoors, at a picnic or a barbecue, for most of us want to make the most of warm sunny days. It continues with several appetizing dishes that are suitable for the middle of the day.

The SPAM Pâté on page 43 is an excellent hors d'oeuvre but it is equally good as a light main course, served with crusty rolls or bread and a salad. When globe artichokes are in season they can be served with this pâté instead of butter, or an oil and vinegar dressing. Scoop out the center choke of the hot or cold artichoke and fill the hole with SPAM Pâté. Try filling raw or cooked small mushrooms or firm ripe tomatoes with the pâté. As you need to scoop out the center pulp from the tomatoes, this could be added to a salad dressing. When you put this pâté with hot foods it melts sufficiently to make a thick flavorsome sauce. There are two very good salads on this page but you can use SPAM, and your imagination, to create many more.

Apple and Beet Salad: Dice equal quantities of cooked skinned beet, unpeeled dessert apples, and SPAM, and mix together. Moisten with a dressing made with equal quantities of yogurt and mayonnaise, and flavored with freshly chopped mint and parsley, and a dash of lemon juice. Serve on a bed of arugula and/or watercress.

Over the years we have experimented with many more mixtures of foods. Once upon a time people felt that meat and fish should never be combined as one dish – now we know better. This mixture of shrimp and SPAM is very good.

Shrimp and SPAM® Salad: Neatly dice 12 ounces SPAM, mix it with 1 cup shelled shrimp, 2 skinned and diced tomatoes, and ¼ cup finely diced cucumber. Moisten with mayonnaise flavored with chopped dill or fennel leaves, and a little white wine or white wine vinegar. Serve on a bed of crisp lettuce and garnish with wedges of lime or lemon.

Making Kebabs

SPAM is an ideal meat to use for kebabs, as it is sufficiently firm not to crumble when threaded on skewers.

SPAM Kebabs: Cut SPAM into 1½–2-inch dice. Thread on long metal skewers with very small tomatoes, portions of green, red, and yellow bell peppers, and small mushrooms. Brush with a little oil or Barbecue Sauce (see below) and cook over the barbecue. Turn once or twice, basting with more oil or sauce. Use tongs – never your hands – to turn the skewers. Take the food off the very hot skewers to eat it.

Barbecue Sauce: Finely chop 1 onion and 2 garlic cloves. Heat 2 tablespoons sunflower oil in a saucepan, add the onion and cook for a few minutes, then add the garlic, along with 2 table-spoons red wine vinegar, 2 tablespoons tomato ketchup, 1 tablespoon brown sugar, 1–2 tea-spoons soy sauce, and 1–2 teaspoons Worcestershire sauce. Heat well then add about 5 tablespoons chicken stock to give the right consistency. Season to taste with salt and pepper. This amount of sauce serves 4–6.

SPAM Satay: While you can use metal skewers for this dish, the meat is generally placed on bamboo sticks (quite easy to obtain from Oriental stores and large supermarkets). New bamboo sticks should be soaked in very hot water before using; this prevents them burning over the barbecue. Satay sauce traditionally contains peanuts so make sure none of your guests is allergic to peanuts, before you serve it.

First make the marinade. Finely chop 1 onion and crush 2 garlic cloves. Add 2 teaspoons crushed and chopped lemon grass or lemon zest, 1 tablespoon sunflower oil, 2 teaspoons soy sauce, a little chopped cilantro, and a pinch of chili powder or 1 small chopped red chile. Cut about 1½ pounds SPAM into 1-inch dice and leave in the marinade for 1 hour. Drain and put on to the sticks. Heat well then serve with Satay Sauce. This dish serves 6–8.

Satay Sauce: Purée 3 tablespoons peanut butter with ¾ cup peanuts (preferably roasted), ⅔ cup coconut milk, 1 tablespoon lime juice, 1 table-spoon brown sugar, 2 teaspoons soy sauce, a little grated ginger root if desired, and salt and pepper to taste. Serve hot or cold.

SPAM® & Pepper Quiche

Preparation time: 30 minutes, plus chilling
Cooking time: 55 minutes
Serves 6–8

Basic pie dough:
½ cup butter
2 cups all-purpose flour, sifted
water, to mix
Filling:
1 red bell pepper, halved and seeded
1 green bell pepper, halved and seeded
1 yellow bell pepper, halved and seeded
7 ounces SPAM®, finely diced
1½ cups Gruyère or Cheddar cheese, grated
3 large eggs or 2 large eggs and 2 egg yolks
1 cup milk
⅔ cup light cream or extra milk
salt and pepper

1   To make the dough, rub the fat into the
    flour until the mixture resembles bread
crumbs. Stir in enough water to make a firm
dough. Knead lightly and chill for 30 minutes.

2   Heat a baking sheet in the oven as this
    helps to crisp the base of the quiche. Roll
out the dough and line a 9–10-inch quiche pan or
dish, at least 1 inch deep. To keep the crust from
swelling, fill the pie shell with a sheet of
foil or waxed paper, and ceramic pie weights or
dried beans. Put the quiche pan on the heated
baking sheet and bake blind in a preheated oven,
400°F, for nearly 15 minutes.

3   Meanwhile, heat the peppers under the
    broiler until the skins blacken. Put them into
a plastic bag. When they are cold, strip away the
skins and chop the pulp finely. Lower the oven
heat to 325°F.

4   Remove the ceramic pie weights or dried
    beans and foil or paper from the pie shell.
Spoon in the SPAM, cheese, and peppers. Beat the
eggs, or eggs and yolks, with the milk and cream,
and salt and pepper. Carefully pour or strain over
the filling. Bake for 40 minutes or until set. Serve
the quiche hot or cold.

Deep SPAM® Pizza

Preparation time: 20 minutes
Cooking time: 30–35 minutes
Serves 1–2

10 inch ready-made pizza base
7 ounces SPAM®, thinly sliced
3½ ounces mozzarella cheese, thinly sliced
2 teaspoons chopped oregano
a few black olives (optional)
2 tablespoons freshly grated Parmesan cheese
Tomato layer:
1 tablespoon olive oil
1 onion, finely sliced
2 garlic cloves, finely chopped
1 cup canned chopped tomatoes
1 tablespoon tomato paste
salt and pepper

1   First make the tomato layer. Heat half the oil in a pan, add the onion and cook for 5 minutes. Add the garlic, tomatoes, tomato paste, and a little salt and pepper and simmer until it becomes a thick puree.

2   Place the pizza base on a preheated baking sheet, brush the inside with the remaining oil, and spread the tomato mixture evenly over the base. Top with the SPAM, sliced mozzarella, oregano, olives, and finally the grated Parmesan. Place in a preheated oven, 425°F, and bake for 15–20 minutes or until piping hot.

Variations: Include a layer of sliced raw or cooked mushrooms, cooked eggplant or zucchini, or red, yellow, or green bell pepper slices with the SPAM.
• Instead of preparing a tomato layer, use about ¼ cup herb-flavored spaghetti sauce or top the pizza base with thinly sliced tomatoes, chopped scallions and/or chives and a little olive oil, then with the SPAM and other ingredients.

SPAM® Fact

The ladies who were engaged to promote SPAM® in song were known as SPAMETTES.

SPAM® Slippers

Preparation time:
25 minutes, plus standing
Cooking time: 35 minutes
Serves 4

2 large eggplants
½ tablespoon olive oil
salt and pepper
Filling:
2 tablespoons olive oil
2 onions, finely chopped
2 garlic cloves, finely chopped
2 large tomatoes, skinned and chopped
12 oz SPAM®
1 teaspoon paprika
1 tablespoon chopped cilantro
Topping:
¼ cup soft bread crumbs
¼ cup grated Gruyère or Cheddar cheese
To garnish:
tomato slices
cilantro sprigs

Did you know?

Stuffed eggplants are often known as 'slippers' because of their shape.

1 Halve the eggplants lengthways, then run a knife around the edges about ¼ inch from the skins. Sprinkle with salt and leave for 30 minutes. Drain away the liquid, rinse in cold water and dry well. Brush the cut surfaces with the ½ tablespoon olive oil.

2 Put the eggplants into a dish, cover with foil and bake in a preheated oven, 400°F, for 20 minutes. Scoop out the soft center part of the eggplants and mash it.

3 Heat the 2 tablespoons oil in a saucepan, add the onions and cook for 5 minutes. Add the garlic and tomatoes and cook for a further 10 minutes. Finely chop three-quarters of the SPAM and add it to the saucepan with the paprika, cilantro, the cooked eggplant pulp, and salt and pepper to taste. Spoon the filling into the eggplant shells and top with the bread crumbs and cheese. Return to the oven for 15 minutes, then serve garnished with the tomato slices, strips of the remaining SPAM, and cilantro sprigs.

SPA

Here's Progress

In SPAM: The History, which begins on page 10, the story of SPAM after the Second World War is described in brief. However, it is interesting to examine in more detail just how the luncheon meat fared for the rest of the 20th century. By the 1950s, SPAM had won rapid renown in the USA and Britain and various other countries during the years of crisis.

The start of the 1950s was still a worrying period, so many countries were suffering from the aftermath of war, refugees needed help to return to their home countries and there were food shortages to be overcome. Britain endured strict rationing up to the end of 1954. SPAM therefore was still a standby for many people, so its sales were high. The surprising thing however was the incredible volume of these sales. The question many people asked was: **'Will this popularity continue, or will it end?'**

In 1959 it was recorded that the **one billionth** can of SPAM was sold, after just 22 years on the market. Since then checks have been kept on its sales worldwide. In 1970 the sales of SPAM reached the **second billion.** In 1980 the **third billion.** In 1986 the **fourth billion.** In 1994 the **fifth billion.** There is the answer **as to whether its popularity endures – SPAM enjoys ever-increasing sales.**

Whenever there are events commemorating the Second World War you can be sure there are displays of SPAM, both in the USA and at the Imperial War Museum in London.

At the present time it is recorded that among 60 million Americans, SPAM is consumed at the rate of 3.6 cans a second. This is equivalent to 216 cans per minute or 12,960 cans per hour.

In Britain, Tulip International, who distribute SPAM from their parent company in Denmark, find they have achieved record sales. Tulip International have a very fine reputation for all their meat products: that is why they were awarded the licence to produce SPAM by Hormel Foods.

In December 1999 a review of the 20th century's top brand-name products in Britain was produced. Fifty names were listed: these covered alcohol, confectionery, dairy products, household items, and groceries, and included the best-known brands of bread, sugar, tea and coffee, together with toiletries.

Within that list was SPAM – a positive proof that the British share the esteem with which the canned luncheon meat is held in so many parts of the world.

Tulip International report that sales of SPAM are growing by 30 per cent, year by year.

Eating Out of Doors

In these days of insulated boxes and bags, picnics can be grand occasions, where a variety of foods may be served at the planned destination with great elegance, or they can be very simple. One of the easiest picnic menus is SPAM with fresh bread or rolls, a selection of simple salad ingredients, and fresh fruit. There is no need to take a can-opener, simply pull the ring at the top of the can of meat and there it is – appetizing pork ready to serve.

For somewhat more elaborate picnics, look at the dishes on pages 23–31 or make SPAMburgers (see page 33) or sandwiches, such as those on page 19. Always remember to take something to drink with your picnic, the fresh air makes you thirsty as well as hungry.

Over the years barbecues have become much less expensive – although there are plenty of luxury models available. This method of outdoor cooking and serving food is extremely popular with both adults and children. It is important that there is plenty of supervision if children are around, for barbecues can become dangerously hot. For successful results, the barbecue must be adequately heated before food is placed over it.

One of the simplest and most popular dishes is **Stuffed Potato Shells.** Prick large well-scrubbed potatoes with a fork, cook over the barbecue (or in the oven or microwave, if this is more convenient), halve or take a slice off the top. Scoop out the potato pulp, mash it with butter or margarine, and season well with salt and pepper. Spoon the filling back into the potato skins, making good center cavities. Fill the cavities with diced SPAM in a cheese, mushroom, pesto, or tomato sauce or Barbecue Sauce (see page 37). Put the potatoes back over the barbecue for a few minutes until they are piping hot. Serve on plates or thick pieces of foil.

Barbecued SPAM: Cut really thick slices of SPAM, brush each side with a little oil or oil and orange juice, and heat over the barbecue. Just before serving, spread the top side with brown sugar or honey. There is no need to turn these slices during cooking. Serve with barbecued mushrooms, tomatoes, and salad. You can brush the slices with Barbecue Sauce (see page 37), before and during cooking.

SPAM®

ED PORK AND HAM

SPAM® Pâté

Preparation time: 15 minutes, plus chilling
Serves 4–6

12 ounces SPAM®
¼ cup butter, melted
2 teaspoons Dijon mustard
2 tablespoons chopped parsley
2 teaspoons chopped basil
6 small sweet dill pickles, thinly sliced
2 tablespoons chopped sun-dried tomatoes
6 black olives, pitted and diced
a little sherry, to moisten
salt and pepper
To serve:
toast
cranberry sauce

1 Mash the SPAM in a bowl, add the hot
butter and the mustard, and mix very well.

2 Stir in the remainder of the ingredients
but take care not to break up the diced
ingredients, for these add color and interest to
the pâté. Add just enough sherry to moisten
the mixture; do not make it too wet – about
1 tablespoon should be sufficient.

3 Spoon into a dish, cover and chill overnight
or for several hours. Turn out and serve
with toast and cranberry sauce.

Variations: Use heavy cream instead of sherry
to give a creamier taste.
• A few raw or lightly cooked and chopped
mushrooms may also be added to the mixture.
• A few skinned pistachio nuts add color and
texture to any pâté.

Did you know?

SPAM® first came on to the
market in 1937. See page 12.

43

Time for Tea

Teatime has been an important feature of the British lifestyle since the 1840s. It is believed that the Duchess of Bedford of that era created the afternoon meal to fill the gap between luncheon and dinner. During recent years, elaborate teas in private homes have almost vanished during the week, but however rushed you may be on week-days, it is worthwhile planning an appetizing tea at the weekend. All the preparations can be made in advance so that the cook, as well as everyone else, can sit back and enjoy a leisurely meal.

Afternoon tea has become the fashion once more in a number of smart hotels. The meal is enjoyed so much that in London, and other large towns and cities, it is advisable to book a table in advance to make sure of being served.

A true afternoon tea menu reflects the traditions of the past. It should include small savory sandwiches (with the crusts cut off, of course); the suggestions on page 19 for interesting sandwich fillings are ideal. There may be plates of wafer-thin bread and butter, and biscuits served with preserves and often with clotted or whipped cream, followed by a selection of cakes and cookies. A choice of teas, such as China, Earl Grey, and Indian, will be offered.

A different kind of teatime meal is still served in many homes, particularly those in the north of England and in Scotland. It is known as high tea and it is very practical where there are younger children. The children get a sustaining meal after coming home from school and well before going to bed. With this kind of tea there is always a savory dish, often cold meat such as SPAM, with salad, plenty of bread and butter, tea, and cakes. Nowadays modern savories, such as a pizza (see page 39) or quiche (see page 38) will be a regular part of the meal and the cakes replaced with fruit of some kind, and maybe a savory cheesecake (see page 23).

Whether your teatime is long and leisurely, or just consists of a quick cup of tea, do make the SPAM Scones on the opposite page. They are delicious and freeze well, so you can make a large batch. We are urged to cut down on sweet dishes and replace these with savory ones. These scones go just as well with coffee as with tea. They will be a popular extra for a packed meal or to take on a picnic.

SPAM® Scones

Preparation time: 10 minutes
Cooking time: 12–15 minutes
Makes 10–12

2 cups all-purpose flour
2 teaspoons baking powder
pinch of salt
2 tablespoons butter or margarine
nearly ⅓ cup **SPAM**®, cut into ⅛-inch dice
about ⅔ cup milk, plus extra for glazing
Filling:
butter or margarine
SPAM®
segments of tomato and cucumber

1 Lightly grease a baking sheet or line it with wax paper. Sift together the flour, baking powder, and salt in a bowl. Rub in the butter or margarine, add the SPAM, and enough milk to make a soft rolling consistency.

2 Roll out the dough on a lightly floured surface to ¾ inch thick. Using a cookie cutter or a glass, cut small circles and brush the tops with the milk. Place the circles on the baking sheet and bake in a preheated oven, 425°F, for 12–15 minutes until the scones feel firm when pressed at the sides.

3 Serve the scones hot with butter. Alternatively, let them cool, then split and spread with a little butter, slices of SPAM, and tomato and cucumber.

Variation: Vegetable Pot Pie: Roast a mixture of vegetables, or make a vegetable casserole. When it is nearly cooked place the scones on top of the hot vegetables and bake as above.

Did you know?

SPAM® cans were used during the war to make dispensing trays. See page 17.

SPAM® for Dinner

Dinner is the most important meal in most households, whether it is eaten at night or in the middle of the day. Nowadays we enjoy a wide range of dishes, including some based on pasta and rice, influenced by the cooking styles of other countries. The dishes selected here should please most people, they are very varied. If you like Oriental stir-frys, turn to page 53 for **Pork & Fruit Stir-fry**, while if you like seafood and rice, there is a wonderful medley of ingredients in the **Penny-wise Paella** on page 50.

One recipe, of the utmost historical importance, is the one for **SPAM® Fritters** on page 59. Undoubtedly this was the most popular dish with young and old in Britain during the Second World War. The liking for fritters of all kinds goes back to ancient Greek and Roman times; that is why I have devoted page 58 to the history of these fried delicacies.

Good cooking takes time and trouble, but most of the dishes in this book can be prepared and cooked within a short time, which is in keeping with our busy modern lifestyle. Some people have very little time to cook and very little space to store equipment and prepare and cook their meals. I refer to those, both young and old, who live in very simple accommodation – possibly on campus or in lodgings while at college or university, or in a small retirement home. There are special ideas to make cooking really easy, starting on page 56.

It is important, however restricted your cooking facilities, to have well-planned and nourishing meals. Eating at home is much cheaper than going to even modest restaurants. SPAM is an inexpensive meat, and provides nutritious protein food at a low cost. Fortunately there are no problems with storage. You can keep the cans in your storecupboard since until it is opened the meat is safe for up to five years.

SPAM® Around the World

SPAM was first launched in 1937 at Austin, Minnesota, USA. For several years after that date it was sold successfully throughout the United States but nowhere else. In 1942 the situation changed with great suddenness. SPAM was sent to Britain to help eke out the limited wartime rations. In addition it went to many spheres of war where the Allied Forces were serving – thus SPAM became known in many very different countries.

When the Second World War ended in 1945 it was apparent that many people in the world were starving so SPAM, with other products, was sent to aid the hungry. Their appreciation was clearly expressed and undoubtedly led to a desire to continue to enjoy what is sometimes known as 'the miracle meat'.

Many American service personnel had been fed SPAM so often that they were less than complimentary. Some vowed never to eat SPAM again when they returned home. Maybe in time they changed their minds and bought SPAM.

As the years passed SPAM reached many more countries. Now the meat is eaten from Alaska to Australia – and from Japan and Korea in the Far East to Canada – and each country gives a special taste to their SPAM dishes. In fact SPAM is sold in 50 countries throughout the world and trade-

marked in 100. It is not sold in Islamic countries for their inhabitants do not eat pork.

SPAM looks the same all round the world, except in Canada and Australia. In Canada the label on cans of SPAM LITE reads SPAM Léger, in deference to the French Canadians, and in Australia it is described as SPAM Spiced Ham instead of Chopped Pork and Ham. However, it tastes just as good all round the world.

SPAM®

Neapolitan SPAM® & Penne

Preparation time: 15 minutes
Cooking time: 20 minutes
Serves 4

2 tablespoons olive oil

1 onion, finely chopped

2 garlic cloves, finely chopped

scant 2 cups canned chopped plum tomatoes

1 tablespoon tomato paste

1 generous cup small white mushrooms

12 ounces SPAM®, cut into narrow sticks

1 tablespoon chopped basil

8 ounces penne pasta

salt and pepper

To garnish:

freshly shredded Parmesan cheese

basil leaves

a few capers (optional)

1 Heat the oil in a large saucepan, add the onion and cook for 5 minutes, then add the garlic and cook for a further 2 minutes. Add the tomatoes and stir in the tomato paste and mushrooms. Cook for 5 minutes, stirring once or twice, then add the SPAM, basil, and salt and pepper to taste. Cook gently for 5–6 minutes.

2 Meanwhile, cook the penne in boiling salted water until tender. Strain, and place in a hot dish. Top with the SPAM mixture, then the Parmesan, basil, and capers, if using.

Variation: Use other pasta shapes such as conchiglie (shells) or farfalle (butterflies). If using longer strands of pasta, dice the SPAM finely.

Cooking Pasta

Always cook pasta in a large pot with plenty of boiling water.

Rice and SPAM®

SPAM adds interest and food value to a number of rice dishes. To turn plain cooked rice into a satisfying dish add chopped herbs, such as parsley, sage, and basil, diced SPAM, and a few skinned chopped tomatoes. Heat with the rice, then serve at once.

The following are more classic dishes.

Mushroom and SPAM® Risotto: Use Italian arborio rice to produce the correct creamy texture. Buy about 8 ounces mushrooms. You can choose all cultivated mushrooms or all wild ones. A mixture of chestnut, shiitake, and oyster mushrooms imparts an interesting appearance and texture. Finely chop 1 onion, wipe the mushrooms, or rinse them in cold water, and slice thickly. Heat 2 tablespoons butter and 1 tablespoon olive oil in a large saucepan. Add the onion and cook gently for 5 minutes. Stir in 1 cup plus 2 tablespoons rice, making sure every grain is coated with fat. Meanwhile, in another saucepan, heat 3¾ cups well-seasoned chicken stock plus a good pinch of saffron threads or powdered saffron. Add about one-third of this hot liquid to the rice with the mushrooms. Stir and cook steadily until all the liquid is absorbed. Continue like this, adding liquid to the rice until the rice is nearly tender. Stir in 8 ounces neatly diced SPAM and 2 tablespoons butter and extra salt and pepper, if you like. Heat well and serve topped with freshly grated Parmesan cheese.
Serves 4

Spicy SPAM® Pilau: Finely chop 2 onions and 2 garlic cloves. Heat 2 tablespoons olive oil in a large saucepan. Add the onions and cook steadily for 5 minutes. Stir in the garlic with ½ teaspoon ground coriander and generous pinches of cumin, chili powder, cinnamon, and turmeric, plus a shake of cayenne pepper. Heat gently for 2 minutes, then stir in 1 cup plus 2 tablespoons long-grain white or brown rice, plus a scant 3 cups chicken stock or water, 3 tablespoons raisins, and 3 tablespoons pine nuts. Simmer steadily until the rice is almost cooked, then stir in 12 ounces neatly diced SPAM and heat thoroughly.
Serves 4–6

Variation: Add a little lemon juice and 2–3 skinned chopped tomatoes to the pilau to enhance the flavor.

Penny-wise Paella

This interesting mixture of meat and fish is one of Spain's outstanding recipes. The cooked dish should be pleasantly moist so a generous amount of stock is required.

Preparation time: 30 minutes
Cooking time: 35 minutes
Serves 4–6

2 tablespoons olive oil
2 onions, finely chopped
2 garlic cloves, finely chopped
1 cup plus 2 tablespoons long-grain rice
3¾ cups chicken stock
½ teaspoon saffron threads or powdered saffron
3 tomatoes, skinned and chopped
1 red bell pepper, cored, seeded, and diced
12 ounces SPAM®, cut into narrow sticks
1½ cups cooked peas
about 18 mussels, cooked and on single shells
about 12 large shrimp, cooked and shelled
salt and pepper

1 Heat the oil in a very large skillet or a paella pan – if you have one. Add the onion and cook for 5 minutes.

2 Add the garlic and cook for 2 minutes, then stir in the rice and continue stirring until each grain is coated with oil.

3 Pour in the chicken stock, then stir in the saffron, tomatoes, red pepper, and salt and pepper to taste. Cook steadily until the rice is almost tender, then add the SPAM and cooked peas. Stir to blend the ingredients and cook for a further 5 minutes. If the mixture is a little too moist, cook fairly vigorously for a few minutes so the excess liquid evaporates.

4 Finally, add the shellfish and heat for just a few minutes, then serve.

Did you know?

Saffron comes from a special crocus and is the most expensive spice in the world.

Chicken Cordon Bleu

SPAM's rich flavor makes it an ideal ingredient to use in stuffings for other meats, chicken and vegetables. In this version of a classic dish it helps to keep lean chicken breasts beautifully moist.

Preparation time: 20 minutes
Cooking time: 15–18 minutes
Serves 4

4 boneless chicken breasts

1 tablespoon flour

1 egg, beaten

about ½ cup soft bread crumbs

¼ cup butter

2 tablespoons sunflower oil

salt and pepper

mixed vegetables, to serve

Filling:

5 ounces SPAM®, mashed

¼ cup grated Gruyère or Cheddar cheese

1 tablespoon light cream

1 teaspoon chopped rosemary

1 tablespoon chopped parsley

1 First make the filling. Mix the SPAM with the other filling ingredients. Form the mixture into a neat shape and cut it into 4 equal portions.

2 Slit the chicken breasts lengthways to make 4 pockets. Insert the SPAM filling into the pockets and press the edges of the chicken together. It is a good idea to hold the edges together with wooden toothpicks while coating and frying them. Remove the toothpicks before you serve the chicken.

3 Mix the flour with salt and pepper and dust the chicken breasts, then coat them with the egg and then the bread crumbs.

4 Heat the butter and oil in a large skillet and brown the chicken portions quickly on all sides. Lower the heat and cook more slowly until tender. Drain on paper towels and serve with mixed vegetables or a salad.

SPAM® Steaks in Port Wine

Preparation time: 10 minutes
Cooking time: 15 minutes
Serves 4

1 bunch of scallions
¼ cup butter
2 teaspoons olive oil
2 cups chestnut mushrooms or a mixture of mushrooms
12 ounces SPAM®, cut into thick slices
¼ cup port
2 teaspoons Dijon mustard
carrot and zucchini ribbons, to serve

1 Trim away and discard the green stalks from the scallions, and roughly chop the white part. Heat the butter and oil in a large skillet, add the scallions and cook until just golden in color.

2 Add the mushrooms, cook for 3 minutes, then remove from the pan with a slotted spoon on to a warmed plate. Put the SPAM steaks into the pan and heat until slightly brown on both sides. Pour the port over the SPAM and add the mustard. Return the scallions and mush-rooms to the pan and heat well.

3 Arrange the scallions and mushrooms on a warmed serving platter and place the SPAM steaks on top. Serve with carrot and zucchini ribbons.

Variation: Flavor the ingredients with a little grated ginger root instead of mustard.

Pork & Fruit Stir-fry

Preparation time: 10 minutes, plus marinating
Cooking time: 12 minutes
Serves 4–6

12 ounces SPAM®

2 large oranges

1 tablespoon oil

1 red onion, finely sliced

3 carrots, cut into batons

2 cups snow peas

1 cup cashew nuts

shredded scallions, to garnish

boiled rice, to serve

Marinade:

8 ounce can pineapple cubes in syrup

½ tablespoon honey

1 teaspoon prepared mustard

2 teaspoons grated orange rind

2 teaspoons lemon juice or vinegar

2 teaspoons soy sauce

2 teaspoons chopped chives

salt and pepper

1 To make the marinade, drain the syrup from the pineapple and measure out 5 tablespoons. Pour the measured syrup into a dish and add the rest of the marinade ingredients.

2 Cut the SPAM into ½-inch slices and then into strips. Place the strips in the marinade and leave for 20 minutes.

3 Cut the peel and pith from the oranges, then cut out the segments – free from skin and seeds.

4 Heat the oil in a wok or skillet. Add the onion and cook for 2 minutes, then add the carrots and stir-fry for 5 minutes. Put in the snow peas and stir for 1 minute, then add the SPAM plus the marinade, the pineapple, oranges, and cashews. Heat thoroughly, then garnish with scallions and serve with rice.

Hawaiian Pork

If you are using canned pineapple rings, use the juice as part of the cooking liquid for the rice.

Preparation time: 20 minutes
Cooking time: 20 minutes
Serves 4–6

1 tablespoon peanut oil
2 onions, chopped
1 green bell pepper, cored, seeded, and diced
1 red bell pepper, cored, seeded, and diced
4 celery stalks, chopped
3 canned water chestnuts, sliced
1 tablespoon cornstarch
1¼ cups chicken stock
1 tablespoon light soy sauce
12 ounces SPAM®, cut into strips about 2 inches long and
   ½ inch thick
5 fresh or canned pineapple rings, each cut into 4 portions
scant 2 cups bean sprouts
salt and pepper
finely sliced lemon zest, to garnish
boiled rice, to serve

1 Heat the oil in a wok or large skillet, add the onions and cook for 5 minutes, then put in the peppers, celery, and water chestnuts and continue stir-frying for a further 5 minutes.

2 Blend the cornstarch with the stock and soy sauce. Add to the pan and stir over the heat until slightly thickened.

3 Put in the SPAM and pineapple and stir-fry for 5 minutes. Finally add the bean sprouts and salt and pepper, and heat for just 1–2 minutes. Garnish with finely sliced lemon zest and serve with boiled rice.

SPAM® Goulash

This is a satisfying stew, based on a classic Hungarian dish. Brands of paprika vary in strength, so add the paprika gradually so you can assess the taste.

Preparation time: 25 minutes
Cooking time: 30 minutes
Serves 4

2 tablespoons olive oil
3 onions, thinly sliced
2 garlic cloves, finely chopped
1 tablespoon paprika, or to taste
2 cups canned chopped plum tomatoes
⅔ cup water
1 pound potatoes, cut into 1-inch slices
12 ounces SPAM®, cut into 1½-inch dice
salt and pepper
bread, to serve
To garnish:
yogurt
flat-leaf parsley sprigs

1 Heat the oil in a large saucepan, add the onions and cook steadily for 5 minutes. Add the garlic and paprika and stir over the heat for 2 minutes. Paprika burns easily, so stirring is important.

2 Add the tomatoes and water, stir, then bring to the boil. Add a little salt and pepper, along with the potatoes. Cover the pan and cook steadily for 10–12 minutes, or until the potatoes are nearly tender.

3 Add the SPAM and cook for a further 5 minutes. Taste and adjust the seasoning, if necessary, then garnish with yogurt and parsley, and serve with bread.

SPAM® Fact

The Hawaiians are keener on SPAM® than any other nation.

Easy Cooking

There are many popular convenience foods on the market – SPAM® being a good example. When time is precious, buy frozen vegetables – there is no preparation and the vitamins are retained. Small bags of mixed salad ingredients are very convenient; you get a variety and save wastage. Make sure your diet includes enough protein and a good proportion of fruit and vegetables.

Meaty Chowder: The term "chowder" has come to mean a soup so full of ingredients that it makes a main dish. Add diced vegetables to your favorite soup; cook until the vegetables are nearly tender, then add diced SPAM and heat thoroughly.
• Serve the chowder topped with chopped herbs. These can be bought chopped and frozen; just take out the amount required.
• If you do not want to prepare fresh garlic, look for available alternatives, including garlic salt.

Pasta Dishes
• Try the recipe for **Neapolitan SPAM® & Penne** on page 48.
• **Eastern Noodles:** Cook and drain the required quantity of pasta and return it to the pan. Add a little peanut butter, whisked eggs and finely chopped SPAM and stir over the heat until the eggs are set. Top with peanuts (make sure no one is allergic to them) and dried coconut.
• For a quick **Italian pasta dish**, heat cooked pasta with chopped fresh or canned tomatoes or pesto sauce, add frozen peas and diced SPAM, and heat well.

Rice Dishes
The rice dishes on page 49 are simple to make and can be varied according to your ingredients.

Pasta and Rice Salads
Cooked pasta and rice are excellent as the basis for salads. Remember these are perishable foods when cooked, so store them only for a limited time in the refrigerator, or freeze them.

If you like pastry dough but find it troublesome to make buy **phyllo pastry dough**. Use oil for brushing the sheets to save melting butter. For a dish to impress your friends make the SPAM Wellington recipe, below.

SPAM® Wellington: Prepare several layers of phyllo pastry dough, according to packet instructions. Spread the center with finely chopped mushrooms blended with a little oil and chopped parsley. Place 12 ounces SPAM in the middle of the mushroom-coated pastry. Fold this around the meat to make a neat parcel and seal firmly. Place on a baking sheet. Make a slit on top, brush with a little more oil and bake for 30–35 minutes in a preheated oven, 400°F, reducing the heat slightly after 20 minutes. Serve hot.

SPAM® Fan Clubs

We are used to hearing about fan clubs, but a fan club for a luncheon meat is certainly unexpected. Nevertheless there are flourishing Official SPAM Fan Clubs in both the USA and in Britain.

How did this happen?

The answer for the USA is provided by Hormel Foods in these words: 'We didn't come up with the idea of a SPAM fan club. People like you did. You sent us photos. You wrote touching stories. You came up with tasty recipes. And more. Why the only thing left for us to do was organize a fan club.'

People joining the Club in the USA pay a $15 annual fee and in return they get a member's shirt, a special certificate, plus a club card and the quarterly newsletter, known as **A Slice of Spam**.

That is certainly not the end of the story, for members are encouraged to make their voices heard by sending in regular contributions about their experiences, special SPAM recipes, and problems to be solved. There are regular events held in the birthplace of SPAM – Austin, Minnesota – and elsewhere. In Anchorage, Alaska, there is a Night Club with a revue, based on Alaskan culture. This includes SPAM mentions and members of the Fan Club enjoy a SPAM menu.

Over the years a special range of merchandise has become available including a **Party Pack**, which includes all the things you will need for a successful SPAM party. There are items of personal wear and pieces of kitchen and sporting equipment as well.

The British SPAM Fan Club was formed fairly recently and it is proving a great success. Membership grows and the fans are enthusiastic about the various activities. There is no charge for joining the British SPAM Fan Club. Several special items, such as T-shirts, ties and earrings, are available for sale to club members.

The regular newsletter is called **The SPAM™tastic Times**. This contains current news items, new recipes based upon SPAM and details of competitions. Recently a lucky fan, who was acclaimed the **SPAMite of the Year**, won a holiday in Hawaii. Members are invited to contribute news and any other items. From one issue of the newsletter I quote a few lines from a poem sent in recently.

SPAM is fab, SPAM is cool
SPAM's enough to make you drool.
Good on toast, good on bread
Brill on earrings that hang from your head,
I've become accustomed to the taste of SPAM.

The History of Fritters

Throughout the ages some form of fritters have been a feature of menus in many parts of the world so it is possible that with the ever-increasing popularity of SPAM, the recipe on page 59 is now made around the globe.

In his book *The Pantropheon*, a history of food in ancient times, published in 1853, Alexis Soyer describes fritters as a delicacy made in Greek and Roman times. These were prepared with flour, kneaded with wine, seasoned with pepper and then worked up with milk and finally with a little fat or oil. Some cooks worked sesame flour with honey and oil and then fried the mixture.

In the 19th century the accomplished cookery writer Eliza Acton gave a recipe for making what she calls Plain Common Fritters, in which a generous proportion of eggs were mixed with flour and milk and fried in hot lard. There is no suggestion in her book that the mixture was used to coat foods. An even better known writer of the same century, Mrs Beeton, gives recipes for a large selection of sweet and savory fritters. She uses various kinds of batter to coat fruit, fish and meat, and the fritters are fried in fat. Today, of course, we use oil for frying in most cases.

One of the greatest chefs of all time, Escoffier, put recipes for various fritter batters in his book *A Guide to Modern Cookery*, published in 1907. On the whole, he favored water or beer, rather than milk, as the liquid in the coating batter.

When one comes to the 1940s, there are many references to **SPAM® Fritters**. These were made by cooks in the Armed Forces, in private homes, but above all else in schools. Ask anyone who was a British schoolchild during the years of rationing (1940–1954) about their favorite school main dish and I have no doubt that in most instances you will be told that it was **SPAM® Fritters**. The basic recipe on page 59 is a good example of the one that would have been made at that time, except that today we can use fresh eggs and fresh milk, rather than the dried varieties. We can also substitute beer for milk – quite a difficult thing to do in the 1940s when beer, although not rationed, was not in plentiful supply. Any on sale was considered essential for drinking but not for cooking.

SPAM

CHOPPED PORK AND HAM

SPAM® Fritters

Preparation time: 10 minutes
Cooking time: 3–6 minutes per batch
Serves 4

12 ounces SPAM®
oil, for frying or deep-frying
scallion mash, to serve
chopped herbs, to garnish
Batter:
1 cup all-purpose flour
pinch of salt
1 large egg
½ cup milk, or milk and water,
    or water or beer

1 Mix together all the batter ingredients in a bowl. The mixture should be thick, in the proportions given above, in order to coat the SPAM well. Cut the SPAM into 8 slices.

2 Meanwhile, heat 2–3 tablespoons oil in a frying pan or wok or heat a depth of oil in a deep-fryer to 340°F or until a cube of day-old bread turns golden in 1 minute.

3 Coat the SPAM slices once or twice with the batter then drop them into the hot oil. If shallow-frying, allow 2–3 minutes on each side; if deep-frying, allow a total cooking time of 3–4 minutes, turning over the fritters as required. Drain on paper towels, garnish with fresh herbs and serve with scallion mash.

Variations: Make the batter with 2 eggs and reduce the liquid by 2 tablespoons.
• For a light "puffy" batter, use 1 teaspoon baking powder, separate the egg(s), and beat the egg whites. Add the yolk(s) to the flour, then the liquid, and lastly the whisked white(s), just before coating the SPAM.
• Add 1 tablespoon oil or melted butter to the batter to give extra crispness.
• Mix cooked corn and diced SPAM with chopped herbs. Add to the batter and fry in spoonfuls.

59

Thai SPAM® Cakes

Preparation time: 15 minutes
Cooking time: 15 minutes
Serves 4

1 pound potatoes, cooked
2 tablespoons butter
3 tablespoons canned coconut milk
2 teaspoons chopped basil
1 tablespoon sunflower oil
1 onion, finely chopped
2 teaspoons Thai green or red curry paste
12 ounces SPAM®, finely diced
pinch of chili powder (optional)
2 teaspoons lime juice
2–3 tablespoons all-purpose flour
3 tablespoons sunflower oil
salt and pepper
To serve:
lime wedges
thinly sliced onion
lime rind

3 Heat the oil in a frying pan, add the SPAM
cakes and fry until crisp and brown on both
sides. Serve with lime wedges, thinly sliced onion
and lime rind.

1 Mash the potatoes with the butter and
coconut milk, add the basil and beat well.
Heat the oil in a saucepan, add the onion and
cook for 5 minutes.

2 Stir in the curry paste, heat for 1 minute,
then blend with the potatoes. Add the
SPAM, chili powder, if using, and lime juice and
season with salt and pepper. Mix thoroughly, then
form into 8 round cakes. Coat with the flour.

Variation: Children's SPAM® Cakes: Mix equal
amounts of mashed potatoes and finely diced or
mashed SPAM. Flavor with herbs or a little tomato ketchup or chutney and form into cakes. Coat
them in flour, then with beaten egg and then with
dried bread crumbs. Fry until crisp and brown.

Hot and Speedy SPAM®

Because SPAM is already cooked it can be heated within minutes. There are many different ways in which it can make a satisfying and interesting hot dish. Here are three suggestions. Each dish serves 4.

Grilled SPAM® and Pineapple: Place fairly thick slices of SPAM from a 12 ounce can on a sheet of foil placed on the rack of a broiler pan. Brush each slice with a few drops of oil or melted butter. Grill under a preheated broiler until very hot and just beginning to brown, then top each slice with a well-drained canned pineapple ring and heat for 2 minutes. Meanwhile, blend the pineapple juice or syrup with arrowroot – allowing 1 teaspoon to each 1 cup. Pour into a saucepan with 1–2 tablespoons dry sherry and stir over the heat until thickened and clear. Serve with the hot SPAM.

SPAM® in Cumberland Sauce: First make the sauce. Grate the rind from ½ lemon and cut the rind from 2 large oranges into matchstick pieces (quite easy to do with a zester or even a potato peeler). Soak the two kinds of rind in 1¼ cups water for 5 minutes. Meanwhile, squeeze the juice from the ½ lemon and the 2 oranges. Put the citrus rind and the water into a saucepan and simmer for 10 minutes, then transfer it to a frying pan. Blend 1 teaspoon arrowroot with the fruit juice and add it to the pan with ¼ cup redcurrant jelly or cranberry jelly, 1 teaspoon prepared English mustard, a good pinch of ground ginger, and 2 tablespoons port. Stir over the heat until slightly thickened. Slice 12 ounces SPAM fairly thinly, add to the pan and poach gently until piping hot. This dish is delicious with young carrots, and rice or new potatoes.

SPAM® in Creamy Mustard Sauce: Blend 2–3 teaspoons mustard powder with ¼ cup flour. Heat 2 tablespoons butter in a large saucepan, stir in the flour then add 1¼ cups milk and ¼ cup light cream. Bring slowly to the boil, stir well and cook until thickened. Slice 12 ounces SPAM, add to the sauce and heat thoroughly. Garnish with parsley, a chopped hard-cooked egg, and crisp croutons (see page 28).
Variation: A few sliced or whole mushrooms can be cooked and added to the mustard sauce with the SPAM.

SPAM® in the Future

At the beginning of the 21st century SPAM is a firm favorite throughout much of the world. In the USA, its parent company, Hormel Foods, LLC., continue to produce vast quantities of this canned luncheon meat, and the enthusiasm for the SPAM Fan Club in that country continues to grow; it is described in more detail on page 57. In Britain SPAM is produced under licence by Tulip International of Denmark and distributed by that company, which is based in Norfolk, England. This firm is noted for their high quality products. The British SPAM Fan Club flourishes: there is more about it on page 57.

Naturally SPAM figures on the Hormel Website and the following information is taken from there.

"This is the one and only official SPAM Website, brought to you by the makers of SPAM Luncheon Meat. All of the others have been created by somebody else. We are not associated with those other websites and are not responsible for their content. As a Company, we are opposed to content that is obscene, vulgar or otherwise not "family friendly." We support positive family values and you can count on us for "safe surfing" by your children."

Recently Hormel Foods, LLC. announced plans for a new SPAM Museum and Visitor Center in downtown Austin.